Letters To My Ex

A Book of Poems
By Jeroberts

ISBN:979-8-9874242-1-6

<u>Dedication</u>

If I never love another,
I hope you know I tried to love you.
We still have forever to go...
If you will have me.
You know who you are.

Table of Contents

Fairytale That Never Ends

I am FOREVER his QUEEN
Our relationship is MAGICAL
We were DESTINED to live...
HAPPILY EVER AFTER
No one knew this day would come
Except the two of us
The day that he found LOVE with me
And I found LOVE with him
Every day is like a DREAM COME TRUE
Every moment spent is ROMANTIC
In every gesture
From him opening doors presented before me
And offering to hold my hand
As I step out of the car or to take a seat
Candlelit dinners served and prepared by him
Catering to my every need
I am his MAJESTY...
Kisses awaken me every morning
Hugs protect me as I sleep

I am his QUEEN...
Every day he reminds me
Our LOVE is MAGICAL...
More BEAUTIFUL
Than a single stemmed red rose
I am his calla lily so pure at heart

2

No evil villain in the night
Will ever come and tear us apart
We have been DESTINED to live
HAPPILY EVER AFTER
Since the day we met
When I found HAPPINESS with him
And he found HAPPINESS with me
Everyday a DREAM of mines has COME TRUE
Every moment I spend with him
I cannot help but return every cater back to you
From running your bath water and bathing you
And offering to feed you
Never letting you forget the extent I will go for you
Moonlit massages prepared by me
Whatever you need from me
Is serviced right at your feet
He is my MAJESTY...
He's FOREVER my KING...
This FAIRYTALE LOVE we share
Will never come to an end

<u>Happiness You Deserve</u>

Knowing that I could never take her place
The chances that I get
Will never amount to nothing
Forever praying…
Don't you wish that I could give you
What you never had

Though times have changed
And tables have turned
Still, I do not stand up
To your moments with her
Fought a thousand days
In so many ways it is all the same
But somehow with her a baby you made

Even though I cannot give you
Something you already had
By now too many kisses
Will not even make things last
In forever…
Always is the dream that we live in
But will not ever come true
Somehow, I got to breathe
Or die without you

And I could never amount to nothing

4

So why should I risk it
By taking this chance
In your life not giving you
This part time romance
If you feel what is real
Then why continue to believe
That I could give you
The happiness you deserve

Knowing I could never take that chance
These times spent with you
Will never amount to nothing
Always wishing...
That you would receive from me
What she never had
As the days ends and the sun goes down
Still, I cannot build up a solid ground
To support the foundation
That you built with her
Knowing that what we tried to build
Will never amount to nothing
Because in her you found
The happiness you deserve

Follow

My heart refuses to **follow** a man
That was never meant for me
Yet, I stand in this place...
By his side
Devoted like I am his wife
Though I know there is no love here for me
Still, I catered to this man every needs
And he devours me so hungrily
Passionately staring at me satisfied
That I remained at his side

My heart refuses to **follow** a man
That was never meant to love me
Yet, two years later I am still standing by his side
Spiritually devoting all my time
Knowing he would never be my husband
And I will never be his wife
Even though I know there are many others
He still returns back to me
Thirsty for more than I can offer him

Still...
Patiently he waits on me
To cater to his every want
And like the fool I have made myself become

I **follow** this man boldly with all of my heart
Hoping that he will see the woman
He has standing by his side...
So devotedly
But he does not...
And now we are back to this place
Where we never begun

I CAN FORGIVE YOU

I CAN FORGIVE YOU!
One day...
Someday...
But not now
It was the fear of losing me
That brought about this doubt in my heart
The man I thought I loved
Betrayed me in the worst way
I care for YOU...
Is the only reason he could muster
To answer my question
As to why I should stick by him
I am so torn...
Confused about if I should leave
Or should I stay and play this waiting game
Broken down because I cannot love him
The way I used to...
My heart just will not let me
But every time I look in his eyes
I wonder who hurts the most between us
No matter how many tears I shed
Over the facts he still asks
"CAN I FORGIVE him"
Maybe one day...
Someday...

But not now

If I walk away now
I wonder if I will feel any regrets
Will my heart love again
Or forever be broken by him
If I stay, I wonder, will I continue to hurt
Over the facts
Be able to move forward with him
In spite of his ultimate betrayal
So deeply torn because no matter
What choice I have to make
At the end of the day, I still love him
Even though I cannot put my finger on why I do
And how much I do
He still asks "CAN I ever FORGIVE him"
One day...
Maybe someday...
But not now

All I CAN think about
Is what they once had
What I thought we had was stronger
One night of unforgivable passion
Turned into an aching in my heart
That defeated me the night it was said
And as much as I tell myself
I cannot get over this I will not move on

I do not want to let him go
He still asks "CAN I FORGIVE him"
What hurts me the most is I know that I CAN
So, I will...

I FORGIVE YOU!

So Hard For Me To Let You Go

It is ***so hard for me to let you go***
But I have to say goodbye
I now know that our relationship
Was built on your lies
And it hurts me to say
That I knew you still loved her
Even before you said it
It just pains me
Because you knew how much I loved you
And you have taken me for granted
Just to still hold ties to the past with her...
The mother of your child...
Your almost wife...
No matter how hard I try to show you
With me there is a better way
You continue to hold on to her
I guess you love her the way I love you
And I cannot believe that once again
I let you hurt me
Held on to your truthful lies for far too long
I guess it is with her instead of me
Is where you should belong

It is ***so hard for me to let you go***
Knowing I am the better woman for you
But I got to say goodbye

11

Because she is the one
Who you really want to be with
The tears I shed are no longer for you
I shed them because I believed in you
That you would not be like
All the others who hurt me
But your lies told the truth all along
That you loved her the way I love you
And it is so extremely hard for me
To hold on now and compete with her
When saying goodbye is so much easier
Than staying in relations with a lie
She has your heart
Is that why you hold on to her
And do not want to let go
I cannot say I wish the best for you
Because I am the better woman for you
So, I will just say goodbye
And let you wonder why I finally left you

I LOVE YOU

I LOVE YOU but I do not know
How to be in LOVE with YOU
Not after all of this…
As much as I try not to build up a guard
To protect me from being hurt again by YOU
My heart continues to betray me
Because it knows that I LOVE YOU

Even though I do not know
How to be in LOVE with YOU
After I forgave YOU for your indiscretion with her
As much as I try to build up a guard
And not focus on what YOU have done to me
My mind continues to betray me
Because all I can think about is how much
I LOVE YOU

But I do not know how to be in LOVE with YOU
After the way YOU hurt me by going back to her
For whatever reason unspoken of by YOU
And as much as my body betrays me
From building up a guard against your touch
I still tremble from your kisses, your hugs
That shows me just how much
I LOVE YOU…

Admittance

I must admit...
I have never known what love felt like until
I met you
You are love in every definition
The feeling I get in my heart
When I am with you warms my soul
A feeling so strange to me
Though I swore I have found love
Many times before
But it has never felt how it feels now with you...
Love

I must admit...
I have never known true happiness until I found you
Though so many experiences before
I believed I was in subliminal happiness
It never felt this way before
The way you are showing me
How happy a woman like me should be at all times
Because a man like you
Is every definition of the word *happiness*

I must admit...
I have never known
What having a wonderful man by my side
Felt like until I dated you

You have been a provider of many things
Above and beyond my expectations
Of things I am used to
You have been a caregiver of my needs first
Never allowing me the chance
To feel neglected or unappreciated
You have been the greatest supporter
Of my accomplishes as well as my failures
A wonderful man you are
In every definition deemed possible
And for all of these things
You have been to me I truly thank you
With love, happiness, and respect
In return for choosing me

I Could Never

I could never make him happy
No matter how hard I try to prove my loyalty to him
Standing by his side
Devoting my all
Like the wife I want to be in his near future
But I know…

I could never make him happy
The life I lead right now cannot supply
The things he wants for
The things he needs for
He receives from me
And all the others he had before me

Even though I was the only one there for him…
Helping him keep a leveled head on his shoulders
And I believed that I will never make him happy
Because he is still in love with somebody else
Even though he vows unconditional love to me

He still wants to lead a single life
With me clinging on to dear life
To show that I will still love him
In spite of the mistakes
He will continue to make

Throughout our relationship
But *I could never* make him happy

Even though he pretends that I do
Just to keep me at bay
But he is only hurting me more and more
Because I know that he can see
That I will never make him happy
Even though I am giving it a try

The World's Greatest

How can I be mad at you for being the man you are
For choosing the women that you chose before me
Every day you give me reasons to believe
You are not faithful to me
With the things that you say
And the actions that you take
I am forever second to the one
· That bared before you life
Third to the life that is your daughter
And waiting...
Hanging...
Swinging on a rope for dear life behind
All the others you placed before me

But how can I be mad at you
For being the man that you are
For choosing all the women you chose before me
The love you give me now
Lacks the passion that used to be
So binding between us
What love I thought I felt for you
I see now was not what you made it out to be
All I know now is that you are hurting me
By being the man, you are and choosing
The women you chose during me

18

The world's greatest lover says he loves me
Says I can have whatever I want
Because I am his lady
But I don't buy it...
Because the world greatest love of mine
Shares his love with everyone excluding me

Sitting In This Room

It is crazy how we can sit in this room
With nothing to say to each other
No how was your day or I missed you
Growing apart is becoming so apparent
Looking at you and wondering
If you are thinking the same
Is the awkward moment
I am being faced with everyday

No one dares to say I love you anymore
It is becoming too far fetched
No attempt at reaching out and rubbing your back
Getting you to embrace me
So that I could feel the warmth
Of your body gracing mine
Or pushing me to grab my attention
Even for a second

I used to waddle in the happiness
That would start an unending battle between us
Fighting for the remote was the best
Knowing that your arms outreached
Farther than mine
Seeing that beautiful smile of yours
While we both laughed at my struggle
Times like that lead to some of our most

Intimate moments
And I loved every minute of it

Sometimes...
Just pausing to take a look
Into those big brown eyes of yours
Saying to myself how much I love this man
Is not even apparent to the naked eye
But still, we sit in this room
He is so unaware of what I may be thinking
His attention so focused on his phone
That he is probably assuming
I am playing a game or texting someone
When I am really deep into my feelings about him

Pouring out my heart in the way that suits me best
Afraid to even ask a question
To start a conversation
Because we will be back to the same point
Where we started
Just sitting in this room...

About Him

I allowed him to hurt me
I am beginning to realize that
But what he does not know
Is that I hear all the smart remarks
He mumbles under his breath
Every word piercing my heart
But I still stay and endure his pain...
His kind of love

Why?
Because I am just a toy to him
Something to be played with
He puts me together then breaks me apart
Making sure he breaks with it
The rest of my broken heart
He knows I love him there is no denying that
I swore to never leave him no matter what
And he uses that to his advantage

I continue to allow him to destroy me
Physically, mentally, and emotionally
The price I pay
To keep the little bit of happiness I have
But what he does not see
Is that he is pushing me away
I am so far away from our relationship

That I don't even see where it went wrong
How did I end up here
Why do I feel like I cannot leave
With those ill-fated words playing on my conscience

Tearing me apart daily when I look into his eyes
I am dying inside, and he is the one killing me
Making me pay the ultimate price
For every female he has dealt with before me
Counting me out every day
But I have stuck by his side through everything

Trying to turn nothing into something
That it will never be
Taking the fall for things I did not deserve
He is making me a bitter woman
Bitter to any man that might come after him
Making it so extremely hard to move on from him
The only man I have ever really loved

WHAT LOVE IS

I am convinced he does not know
WHAT LOVE IS
He does not realize that LOVE does not say
All the hurtful things that he says when he is mad
Then try to take it all back
And expect me to forget and forgive it all

He does not realize
That LOVE does not say
How it hates kids that are not his
No man should ever say those words
To a woman he claims to LOVE
Because to LOVE her is to love her kids too

But he does not realize...
That LOVE does not
Get mad and strike a mighty blow
One so painful that it left me in shock
Thinking about all the times
He said he would never lay a hand on me
He would never hurt me in such a way
Still...

I am convinced that he does not know
WHAT LOVE IS

24

Because what he feels is not LOVE at all
And I do not know
What kind of LOVE he has had before me
I know that LOVE does not tear me down
And then try to build me back up
Belittle my worth
Because it does not live up to his standards
Say how great of a woman,
A mother I am then take it all back
And slander me with all the things that I lack

LOVE does not cheat on me and creates life
Then lie to me about never wanting the child
When he really did...
Not once but twice
And if he had to do it all over,
I just know he will do it again
Because he was never sorry for doing it
To begin with

LOVE does not entertain other women
Just because I lack things that he expects of me
But the very things I lack
Are the things he turns a deaf ear to
When I express the way, I feel.
He says he listens to me,
But I know he is just finding things
To hold against me

I am so convinced that every I LOVE you
Does not mean a thing to him
Because deep down in my heart
He does not LOVE me like he says he do

LOVE does not nor has it ever been this way before
But I am convinced that I LOVE him,
And this is what I am in this relationship for
But now that we are nearing the end,
I realized what my mother once told me
That I really do not know WHAT LOVE IS

Unwritten Book

Sitting here thinking how I could
Write this relationship in a book
A page turning thriller
Of how dating you actually looked
This sweet disaster including in depth
Of how the beginning never showed its beauty
And how chapter after chapter
Your sinister ways
Lead to my untimely unhappily ever after
No one to warn me about the hidden truth
Behind your devilish charm
Though I must admit it was your charm
That continued to entangle me in your web
Of lies, secrets and deceit
Foolish was I to remain hoping
That I could get you to change
And the longer I stayed what hope that was left
In me slowly began to fade
Normally turning to pen and paper
Released me of the misery I contained
But even my thoughts
Somehow became constrained
Could not figure out how to be happy...
Not knowing how happiness looked
I could not show vulnerability through tears
Of the passing years

Because my heart like a fish had been hooked
Do not know how to give up and walk away
Cannot find it in my soul to stay
I said it over and over
He does not know what love is
And why everything now is only about him
It was all just a fantasy too beautiful to be true
The best seller I have never wrote
Was lived out through you

Commemorative Speech

There is a lot of words I would like to say
To **commemorate** you.
To express how grateful, I am to you
For being a part of this moment in time.

I want to start off by saying I thank you.
I thank you because without you
I would not have tried to pick up where I left off.
I would not have the courage to continue
This journey that I started so many years ago.
I want to thank you for never giving up on me
Even when I had given up on myself completely.
For pushing me to see my own worth,
For knowing that I could do this.

Thank you for being my support system
Cheering on my every accomplishment
And understanding my failures.
Always talking to me, always encouraging me
To see things from a different perspective.
Even though you will not take full credit
For pushing my drive.
I still thank you for being there

Listening to me complain
About the amount of work I had to complete.
Giving me your perspective on the many challenges
I faced trying to get this far.
For all the things that seem like it was not nothing
Meant everything to me.

I **commemorate** you for helping me get here...
Where I am at now.
I do not have to say your name
Because you know who you are.
I am thankful for you
And your words of encouragement.
I am also thankful for the times
I felt like you were being hard on me.
You have been my biggest inspiration
Seeing me through
To one of my biggest accomplishments.
I cannot find any other way
To show my appreciation than writing this for you.
I will always **commemorate** you.

NEW YEAR

Every NEW YEAR I hope for a greater you.
A man who admits his flaws and recreates himself.
Not for perfection but to show that he is ready
To grow along side of me.
Standing together and letting go all of the things
That is holding us back from being greater together.
Making power moves instead of drowning
In a sea of inevitable possibilities.

Every NEW YEAR
I hope for a better relationship with you.
Better communication between us.
Accepting those moments
Of disagreeing and improving on it.
But every NEW YEAR it is the same.
The same temperament I despise.
Being used as a defense mechanism to protect you
From previous attacks from your past relationships.
The same lack in effort is still present.
Never giving a second thought to my feelings
Still protecting your own.
Too many YEARS in and I am still waiting
For a change

In the NEW YEAR with us.
Resolutions we have set forth

But dare not to discuss.
Problems we want to change
But refuse to get out of our comforts.
The NEW YEAR comes and goes, and we are still
Wondering how we have made it this far.
With everything that is meant to tear us down
As a whole breaks us apart individually.
Nothing to regret, nothing left to chance.
Just a NEW YEAR in a relationship
That needs to be made brand NEW.
So that you can love me as I love you.

Every NEW YEAR I look at you wondering,
If this is going to be the YEAR worth fighting for.
Worth holding on to you
And continuing this journey.
Or is it finally time to stop this clock
And start the NEW YEAR going our separate ways.

Greater Man

I used to dream of a future
With no broken promises and no lies.
I used to believe I wanted a future with him
But now that future has shattered before my eyes.
The ***man*** that I believed he was,
Was truly an angel in disguise.
And for the past years all he has done
Is made my heart cry.

I accepted who he was.
I even saw the ***man*** he was trying to be.
I thought I was seeing all of these things,
But he was a mirage...
The ***man*** of my fantasies.
Becoming a ***greater man*** for someone else.
That someone else that he led me to believe
He had let go.
That someone else we used to fight about
Years ago.
While he was chasing a lifestyle,
But I see that he is still in love...
With her...
His past.
The past that did not last
Because he was too busy trying to be.

33

A *__greater man__* for someone else...
That someone else just was not me.

But I fought a great fight
Justifying all the things that he said.
The promises he did not keep.
The poems to him he never read.
Wondering when did I become so gullible.
When did I fall so weak for this *__man__*?
Fearing that I cannot let him go.
Do I want to?
A part of me says yes.
But there is something else that is telling me no.
A constant battle of what is best for me.
And I was hoping it was him.
I used to believe that I loved him.
Now I long for the opportunity to let him go.

Throwing away years of unfaithfulness...
I just have to let go.
I no longer know who I am with him.
Nor do I want to know.
Because the *__man__*
Who spent all these years with me.
Was becoming a *__greater man__* for someone else.

Family Divided

For years I have been fighting to make us a whole
Instead, we have been living in a divided home
There is you and your kids then me and mine
All I want is for our families to be combined
                    Together...

Like how you once said
We would have forever to go
But these past years I have watched
As we've both grown...
Further away from each other
Because we have differences
That we cannot seem to set aside
To raise our children
                    Together...

A statement that we will never be...
Because I swear you do not know the first thing
About being a family
So quick to leave mines behind
And worry about your own
I just do not understand how you can treat mines
Like they do not belong
                    Together...

With you, with your kids

But you expect me to accept you as a man
When you cannot accept my children
All I ever wanted was that picture perfect portrait
Of what a family supposed to be
With a family divided that will never be

I Don't Know How To Let You Go

I could not dare face you…
And say that I don't love you anymore
Because I do that is the part that hurts the most
I am still in love with you
And I don't understand why
You can hurt me a million times
And I will still walk back into your arms
Because I don't know how to let you go

I can say I am done with you
Until I am blue in the face
But once I look into your eyes
That strength to walk away
Fades…
My heart beats for you once more
And I cannot tell it to stop
I don't want it to
Because I don't know how to let you go

It is the sad truth what love allows us to go through
To allow you to dance with my heart once more
Even when I am falling apart before you
It is as if I lost myself within you somewhere
An ever-changing maze
That I don't know how to let go

CHOOSE

How can a man fix his mouth
To tell a woman he is supposed to love
To CHOOSE…
Between the child she has carried
In her body, loves, and nurtured
And him...
Someone she had to learn to love
It is so selfish of him to think
He has the right to make her CHOOSE...
Her children have always been first in her life
They are always there to pick up the broken pieces
Of her when the man decides to leave
He knows that they are a package deal
To love her is to love her children
Even when the children are not his

A man cannot force a woman to CHOOSE...
Between loving him...
A coward who will CHOOSE
To come and go as he sees fit
And loving her child who has been a part of her life
And continues to be a part of her life
Long after he has gone

All women are not the same,
There are some who would lose everything

38

To chase after a man
I would never be that type of woman
I CHOOSE my children over any man
Their happiness is my responsibility
So, to answer your question
Of who do I CHOOSE...
I CHOSE them.
My son's

I am ready to walk away from years
Of feeling like I had to CHOOSE...
Years of talking to and reminding them that I will
CHOOSE them over anything
Even life...
They are what fuels me to keep pushing forward
They are my choice
Even when my last breath is taken
I will never again allow a selfish man to tell me to
CHOOSE...

Where Did We Go Wrong

Looking back
All the warning labels were overlooked
I read differently...
All the qualities that made up you
Did not want to pass judgment and get judged too
And you did with every disagreement...
Without shedding light on the facts
That you have been hurt too
Not by me, but others...
That is who you began to see me as
Her,
Her,
And her...
Regardless of the fact that we had no similarities
Other than the common denominator
You...

Your past became my past
Fast forwarded to the future
A future now gone...
A future without you
I loved you for all the wrong reasons
Because I thought you would do the same
Yet, we...
Me,
Her,

40

And her were the problems you blamed
But I never turned my back on you
Never left you
Even as you demanded me to choose
Fought for all the warning labels
I saw the reds, wore the blacks,
And lived the blues...
That was my fault

Finally, I am accepting part blame
Not because I did not want to see the warning signs
But because after all these years
I could never make you change

I'M NOT AFRAID OF LOSING YOU

I would give all of this up
For a real chance at love
At happiness…
At forever…
Things I have been begging for
That I deserve
That would never come from loving YOU
Am I ashamed?
When I know I gave YOU the absolute best
I am the absolute best woman for YOU
After all this mess I have been wiping away
Bagging up and throwing it away

I'M NOT AFRAID OF walking away
NOT this time or the last time
Or from the very beginning

I'M NOT AFRAID to say I have cried over YOU,
Over myself, over this relationship
Because I had been through
The worst in YOU, the best that has yet to come
And after all of it I was never AFRAID

To walk alone...
I had been alone for years
Watched as YOU worked alone...

42

Without me
Listened as YOU talked OF futures NOT with me
Heard heart breaking words being spit in my face

So many years of being alone with YOU
YOU became the "I" in team, the "YOU" in us
Never thought that in this very place I would be
YOU questioning my being here,
There,
Everywhere except with YOU
Which is why I'M NOT AFRAID OF LOSING YOU

CRAVE

I wonder how much longer I will **_CRAVE_** your touch
Your strong embrace that drives me wild
Now that it is over...
The sexual chemistry we shared was unmatched
Our bodies so compatible, so easily entwined
So hard to fight the emotions of my body
When it knows the care and concerns that you can
provide

How can I mentally prepare myself for the end
When you continued to take my body
Up until the last day
Begging for this not to be how it ends
I do not want the feeling to stop
The **_CRAVING_** to cease...

As time goes on, I am sure the memories will fade
The love will go away
As long as I do not see your face
And remember the way you made my body shiver
Just a touch would release a river flow
Of passion, hunger, and desire for you
That I can no longer **_CRAVE_**

NOTHING WORTH SAVING

There's *NOTHING WORTH SAVING*...
His final words to me
As he turned to say as for us, I love you...
But that did not stop him
From closing the chapters in our book
Now putting both feet out of this relationship
He finally gave up
On me...
On us...
After so many years of stating he was not ready to
Now the tables have turned
And I am not ready

I believe I could accept living in separate
households and continuing on
But that is not what he wants
How can he not feel the same
Separation anxiety as I do
We have been together for far too long
For him not to feel the incompleteness
The emptiness
The tearing of his heart strings
Not waking up every morning next to me
The love of his life of 10 years
But there's *NOTHING* left
To put the pieces back together again

NOTHING left to give it one more try
Did we even try?
Just a back and forth blame game
That pushed us farther apart than we were
Scattered fragments of him and me
That could not be *SAVED*

Unfillable Void

I cannot stand to look you in your face
All the old feelings come rushing back
Memories have turned into emotions
Trickling down my face
And I am not sad
Just remembering the parts of me that I lost
While I was with you
Cannot stand to see the questioning
In your expressions
Your eyes searching my soul
But there is nothing to find
You left me so long ago
I did not realize your absence
Until I was ready to leave
I thought I was in love
And you were my person
Only to realize we were trying to fill
Unfillable voids in each other

OUR WORLD

OUR WORLD has stopped spinning
But we continue to act on selfish desires
My need of you is much more personal
Than your need for me
I long to be what makes you a whole
With only you...
My better half
A feeling I have been begging for
Feelings my mind cannot comprehend
My heart can no longer mend
Not this time...
I feel used up
Damaged and depleted
Yet, these selfish needs desire you more
And I feel so stupid lying under you
Enduring the pain, I cannot seem to let go of
Once more...
So many times over
Watching OUR WORLD burn
To the unstable foundation it was built on
Letting you walk out of my life for the final time
So many points we have been beyond return
But we continue to act like the end was not near
There is nothing left to fear
In OUR WORLD

OVER

This is **OVER**

Yet, he leads me to believe it is not

How can you continue to harbor feelings for me

When your heart is not in it

You can love me for who I was to you

But refuse to stand by me

When the odds are against me

I can no longer pretend this is not happening

Believe that it is going to continue to be you and me

This is **OVER**...

Yet, he does not know if he wants it to be

HURT

My heart still in this
There is no way I can let you go
I thought that I could
The love I have for you will not release me
And the fight in me will not give you up
Even as I watch you back down
Preparing to throw in the towel
Nothing is clear to me
As I continue to take swings at this HURT
He continues to block my every blow
Allowing me to beat myself up
Again, and again
Never throwing in the towel
Knocking me down every round
I cannot lose to this HURT
My heart still with him
I will not let you go
I just cannot
Because it HURTS

Remember

I keep having flashbacks from last night
Biting my lip...
Remembering
So much intensity
So much passion, emotions, electricity
That a rush runs through my body that I cannot
shake
You have me lost in a zone
Oh, how I want you badly right now
Satisfying you in that moment brought out the
animal in me
Staring at you ready to devour every inch of you
Fiending for your lips pressed against mine
Our tongues to dance
Your strong arms to wrap around my body
I could not wait to taste you
I crave for you like a drug
You are my addiction
And my body belongs to you and only you
Because I know what you are capable of
The driving force that penetrates my love so deeply
that I cannot escape it
Biting my lip once more as you slowly caress my
body into one explosion after another
Remembering the look in your eyes

51

As we listened to my river of emotions continuing to
run deep...
For you
I am so taken over by this feeling that my body
makes me **remember**
Every sweet convulsion that took me over
Holding me so I could not escape the pleasure
once more
I want you so badly
Shaking with anticipation
Look what you have done to me
My toes curl as **I remember**

I Miss Us

I miss us like this
It is so noticeably clear
Our passion for one another runs deep
The twinkle still dances in our eyes
When our souls meet
I miss us
I miss this...

The way you would do anything
To put a smile on my face
All of our play fights
Turned into the most intimate embrace
The moments when I needed you the most
You hugged me out the blue
You have been
My lover, my companion, my best friend,
And *I miss* you

For so many years...
I cannot believe we ended like this
There are still so many things that I do *miss*
I want to call you and reminisce
About the way we would challenge each other
Your random moments
Of pulling me to dance with you

The way you used to adjust your height to mock me
Your kisses while I sleep
Pulling me to you to lay my head on your chest
You were the absolute best
There is still more to *miss* if we could get through
All the barriers...
I cannot believe you got me like this
Missing us

EMPTY

As I flip through
The EMPTY pages of my notebook
I feel just as EMPTY
As your love has made me
The more I turn the pages
The more I realize that you never loved me
Before I would fill these pages with tears
With hope, with dreams, with heartbreak
Depicting our love story
Wishing that you would read it and save us
Even though it was me that was drowning
In this sea of romance

We Were

We were everything together

Each other's peace

Happiness was always within reach

We were in love without end

The best of friends

Companions

We were...

The right hand to each other's left

And then he left

What ***we were***...

Letter To My Ex

To whom this may concern:

But you know who you are. I do not want to write about you forever. It is time to finally let go. What we had was gone long before we started. I no longer feel brokenhearted. I do not want to look back at these words someday and shed tears. Reminiscing about how toxic loving you has made me. I want to create new memories without you interfering in it. Truly be happy... Grow into love with someone new. Leaving behind the baggage you stored in my heart. Putting back the pieces of me that fell apart. I thank you for my past, it has created a beautiful future. Cheers to the end of me and you...

Wanting You

I want you so bad
It is hard to fight my urges
To kiss your full lips
Caress your man hood to erection
Straddle your girth
And ride this wave of ecstasy
To the brink of explosion
What have you done to me
I crave you so much
That my body tingles at the thought of you
Caressing my breast
Gripping my ass and thighs
Pushing my legs apart
To dip your fingers into my cookie jar
Diving tongue deep into my ocean
Flooding the sheets with pools of juices
It is so hard to stop this
Thoughts of you racing through my being
Squeezing my legs so tight to fight this feeling
Of wanting you every hour of the day
I do not ever want this feeling to go away
Of wanting you...
So badly

I'm Not Ready For Alone

Sleepless nights
With a bed full of pillows
Missing the body
I used to come home to
Was not prepared to see him go
I could not watch him leave
All he left
Was my head full of dreams
Future endeavors
Disappeared like his things
Pictures left behind
Still tugging at my heartstrings
I do not want this
I am not ready for alone...
Miss hearing his laughter
His voice on my phone
This place feels so empty
Without him with me
But this had to happen
He had to leave
It was better for him
I cannot say the same for me
To be in love at a distance
Is too much to bear
I am not ready for this
Alone after so many years

YOU

I cannot keep thoughts of YOU
Out of my head
YOU imprinted a burning passion for YOU
Within my soul
That no other man can fill
It is like YOU want to keep
YOUR hold on me
Long after YOU left us
Flashbacks of YOUR touch
Continues to take my breath away
Possessing me to touch myself the way
YOU used to
So lost in my head
In my body
Within my soul
Waiting on YOU to release me
Back into the sea of fishes
Waiting to be captured by YOU

Caged Bird

Am I a *caged bird*
Or will you finally set me free
Free of the binding chains
That I wear like bracelets on my wrist
Forever trapped in my love for you
Patiently waiting for you to decide
If you want me to continue on this fantasy ride
With you

So, am I a *caged bird*
Or will you finally set me free
So confused by your actions
Taking control of me
Keeping me tangled in a web
Struggling to be free
Of you

Am I a *caged bird*
Trapped...
Until the day you release me
And no longer feed me lies, broken promises
Marriage proposals that will never come

Keeping me *caged* in your heart
As you build a wall around it to close me in
Never giving another a key
Like the one you gave me

The *caged bird*...
Waiting to be set free

Pressured

He loves me...
But not enough to make me his wife
He loved the way I catered to him in the beginning
Doing everything a good woman should
But not enough to make me his wife

Spent so many years together
Giving me the title but never provided the ring
So, I changed...
Catered to him less and being a girlfriend more
Questioning
What I am staying in this relationship for
Because he loves me
But not enough to make me his wife

He is noticing the change
Wanting me to return to who I used to be
In the beginning...
Talks of marriage has become being pressured
Even though no pressure is being applied
Just want him to know I am serious about us
And I want to be the one by his side
His parents have been married for years
Yet, marriage holds no value to him
Just a ring and a piece of paper
A waste of money being spent

63

So, I am walking away...
From being in a marriage less relationship forever
Even though he loves
But not enough to be his wife

Morning Kiss

In search of the *morning kisses*

That used to greet me daily

They went away so abruptly

I could not savor the feeling

The happiness that spread across my lips

Knowing this man loves me

Enough to still *kiss* me

Even as he is saying his final goodbye

BreakUp

I never thought a *breakup* would hurt this much
Got me feeling like I never meant a thing to him
I am feeling like I was not enough
Seeing so many happy couples
And marriage proposals
Wondering why such things never happened to me
He got me feeling like I was not good enough
Even though I had given him a decade of my life
Felt like I was so much more than a wife
He was my life partner
But he broke my heart too many times
This time beyond repair
Not understanding why my heart cares
We *broke up*
And I cannot move on past him
Nobody would ever measure up to what he was
I refuse to give another 10 years
That leads to nothing
That leads to another *breakup* that hurt so much

<u>Wells</u>

Eyes <u>welled</u> with tears
That I refuse to let fall down my face
Once again, I am in my feelings
And my heart is displaced
Cannot figure out how to ease the pain
While I drink my sorrows away
He was the world to me
My drug...
I got a high every time we locked eyes
For once I was in love
He was my protection when we embraced
I loved looking at his beautiful face
Lost in my hopes that he will return to me
That he will still want to be...
What we can no longer be, which is together
Did we ever mean anything to each other
Or were we just a crutch
Holding each other up for disappointment
While so many years were wasted...
Spending so much time
Repairing damages from the past
That we could not last
Past the memories lining the <u>wells</u> of my eyes
To disguise the heartbreak
From showing on my face

Searching

I keep looking for something

That is not there

The more I **search** the more I yearn

For you to magically appear

Hoping your **searching** for me too

With wide open arms

Anticipating our return

Back to each other

To continue on to forever

Because that is how much longer

We have to go

I HATE That I Love You

I HATE that I love you
I HATE that memories
Bring all the old feelings back
Talks of us ending just open new scars
I am not over you which is apparent
I was so very much in love with you it is sickening

I HATE that I cannot let us go
I HATE that you continued
To pretend like we were not over
Continued to keep me involved
Making love to me like you still had a burning desire
To be close to me
Which made the end so confusing
Because you left me unsure
Of what you really wanted to do about us

I HATE that you did not keep your word
When you said it was over
I HATE that you were willing to try to continue
Did you really?
Or was it just that you wanted to prove
That you were done
But appeased my selfish feelings
Of not wanting to let go
Not wanting to walk away from you,

The 10 years we built,
The forever to go
The promise of marriage coming
But in reality, you wanted to let all of this go

I HATE that I love you
I HATE that I cannot let you go
I HATE that you want to
I HATE that I don't…

SHE STILL WANTS YOU

SHE STILL WANTS
To feel YOUR body wrapped around hers
YOUR lips to press against hers
Tongue to slither around her neck
SHE STILL feels YOU like YOU never left
YOUR fingers swirling into her nectar
YOUR eyes piercing her soul as YOU enter her
YOUR stroke so powerful
It makes her weak lying under YOU
YOUR deeper embrace inside her
It makes her lose control of her lady juices

SHE STILL WANTS to feel the slight grip
Around her throat as YOU dive deeper
YOUR vice to whisper in her ears
YOUR kisses to smother her moans
And SHE moans how SHE STILL WANTS YOU...

SHE STILL WANTS YOUR tongue to lick her clean
YOUR mouth to suck her soul from her body
To see the look in YOUR eyes
As SHE escapes to ecstasy
SHE STILL WANTS YOU

But YOU'RE not there
SHE STILL pulsates at the thought of YOU

71

SHE STILL wraps her legs tight around her pillow
To fight off WANTING YOU
SHE knows SHE can no longer have YOU
Yet, SHE STILL WANTS YOU

SMELL OF HIM

The **SMELL OF HIM** lingers
No matter how many times
I try to rid my body OF HIS SCENT
It remains…
So, intoxicating
So, suffocating
Smothering me daily
I cannot get rid **OF HIM**
HIS **SMELL** lingers on everything
A permanent STENCH
That marked its territory within my nostrils
I guess losing **HIM** was not enough
The **SMELL OF HIM** lingers to drive me
insane
And it remains…
Long after HE left me

Free... At Last

I forgive you...
Was like a breath of fresh air
Escaping my lips
And the weight I carried
Finally
Lifted from my shoulders
I am *free*...
At last, the pain no longer hinders me
The love I have for you
Has broken the spell it cast
Free... at last
To love again

Thank You

for reading my poetic thoughts….

Getting to this point has been a long journey of self-doubt, fear of lack of support, rejection, etc. Most things a new writer goes through when submitting a manuscript. This is not the end…

Stay tuned for my next books:

All Because Two People Fell In Love

and

Jus Me… Dropping The T

Bonus Poem

Do You Love Me Still

Can you fix your mouth to say
The words I want to hear
Daily I go about my day
With my heart full of fear
Kisses still placed on my forehead
Tells me you still care
Asking for those three favorite words...
I would not dare
To recite them and not hear them said back
Yet, our chemistry is still strong
And does not appear to lack
Passion...
Desire...
The hunger to be entwined
In each other's arms
By asking this of you…
I swear I mean no harm
I want so bad to hear you say it
I fear another feeling has replaced it
Anguish...
Hurt...

Lusting for another chance
To be locked in your embrace
To hear the words
Your mine...

You belong to me...
Looking into your eyes
Bowing my head
Too embarrassed to realize
The emotions building
Voice shaking with uncertainty
Heart racing from 0 to 100
Mind jumping around still wondering
The look in your eyes are searching
Anticipation turns into impatience
Words stumbling about
Too afraid to carry this mission out
But I want to hear you say does words
I pray my feelings will not be curved
Enlighten me with the will to ask
Do you love me still...

About The Author

Jessica Roberts is a Florida native, born in Fort Myers, and is a mother of two young men. She began writing poems at the age of thirteen. She has handwritten three unpublished books: Nothin' But Drama completed in 2002, Misery Luvs Company completed in 2003 & And Da Drama Neva Ends completed in 2004 while attending high school.

 Jessica has centered her writings on different experiences, but her main focus is to express her thoughts on different forms of relationships, heartbreak and more through poetry. Her first book Letters To My Ex was published September2002 with Amazon. She then revised her book and republished it through her own publishing company as well as her newest release All Because Two People Fell In Love published in January 2023.

 When Jessica is not writing, she is an Event Planner at her company Jessica's Party Planning, she is also an avid reader. Some of her favorite authors include Carl Weber, Mary B. Morrison, Anna J, and Ashley and JaQuavis. She loves listening to various genres of music and also enjoys watching Horror movies.

Other Books by Jeroberts

Letters To My Ex Paperback
ISBN: 979-8-9874242-1-6
Letters To My Ex Hardcover
ISBN:979-8-9874242-9-2
(Available on Amazon, Barnes & Noble and
Google Play Books)

All Because Two People Fell In Love Hardcover
ISBN: 979-8-9874242-2-3
All Because Two People Fell In Love Paperback
ISBN: 979-8-9874242-0-9
(Available on Amazon, Barnes & Noble and
Google Play Books)

Coming Soon…

Jus Me… Dropping The T Paperback
ISBN: 979-8-9874242-3-0
Jus Me… Dropping The T Hardcover
ISBN: 979-8-98742-4-2
(Available on Amazon, Barnes & Noble and
Google Play Books)

Nothin' But Drama December 2023
ISBN: 979-8-9874242-5-4
Misery Luvs Company March 2024
ISBN: 979-8-9874242-6-1
The Misperception of Everything July 2024

Letters To My Ex

Follow Jeroberts Poetry
on social media platforms such as:

Blogger:
jerobertsthoughts.blogspot.com/
Facebook:
Facebook.com/jerobertsthoughts
Instagram:
instagram.com/1tsjessibaby/
Hive: @authorjeroberts
Medium:
medium.com/@jerobertsthoughts
Reddit:
reddit.com/user/Jerobertsthoughts
Pinterest:
pinterest.com/jerobertsthoughts/
Tumblr:
tumblr.com/blog/jerobertsthoughts
TikTok:
tiktok.com/@jerobertsthoughts
Twitter:
twitter.com/Jerobertspoetry
Goodreads:
goodreads.com/jerobertsthoughts

Letters To My Ex

Made in the USA
Columbia, SC
27 December 2023

29457945R00052